Wild Woman's Guide to Etiquette:

Saving the World One Handshake at a Time

Sharon Hill

Online editions may also be available for this title. For more information visit http://www.lulu.com.

Acknowledgements

To My Beloved Elmer,
My Husband, My Friend

Table of Contents

Introduction

True or false? Everyone wants to make a positive impression. Everyone wants to be admired and respected for their social skills.

If you answered true, that's cool. But if you answered false, it could mean you are a right-brained, logical thinker who doesn't care what people think about you. You are satisfied with yourself and do not require the approval of others.

Regardless of your answer, the fact is that people who demonstrate confidence and proper etiquette have an advantage over people who don't. Etiquette can get you ahead in business, help you win negotiations, and leave a positive impression on people that you may not even know are watching you. These skills can help you land a job, get a promotion, make an impression on that lady or gentleman you've got your eye on, assist with public speaking, and give others pride in being a reference for you for various opportunities.

This book is for those in need of basic etiquette and those who want to polish their skills. It is for people who want to avoid looking foolish in social situations and want to be admired for showing class and confidence.

Etiquette is a state of mind more so than a series of rules to be followed. Without the proper mindset, you just go through the motions. With a proper frame of mind, centered on others as opposed to yourself, etiquette becomes a natural extension of how you wish to be treated.

Difference between Etiquette and Manners

Etiquette is protocol. It includes rules of behavior that you memorize; it seldom allows for personal variations, individual concerns and needs. This book focuses on that protocol. However, I also pay attention to manners. Manners relate to kindness and caring about others. According to Linda Reece, author of "Good Manners & Etiquette For Everyday Living" having good manners goes beyond socially acceptable behavior and relates more to how you treat others because you care about them, their self-esteem and their feelings. Good manners are under your control because they come from your heart, not from a formal etiquette book like this one.

Linda Reece writes further that good manners form the basis for good human relationships wherever you are—at home, at work, at the grocery store, in church, in an airport or on the golf course.

More and more business people are faced with the challenges of knowing acceptable or expected etiquette for today's business world. Real manners are instinctive. You don't turn then on and off like a switch. Real manners include such things as:

- Becoming comfortable at making introductions and being introduced—and making others feel good while it's happening. (Chapter 4. Introductions)
- Becoming comfortable with good table manners (Chapter 13. Upscale Dining) and the art of "Small Talk with Strangers" so that you can concentrate on others and what they are saying. (Chapter 5. Small Talk with Strangers)
- Noticing the "wallflower" at a social event and helping to bring that person into the group (Chapter 5. Small Talk with Strangers)

Don't forget that your own family is important, too. Setting a good example and practicing good manners within your home helps to create a more pleasant atmosphere and enables everyone to become more aware of their personal behavior. They'll also feel more at ease with their social skills when outside their home surroundings.

Good manners can be contagious. When you're kind to someone else, that person returns your kindness. Two people then feel good about themselves and each other and spread this good feeling to others. We should never be too busy for kindness and caring.

With "good sense" etiquette and caring manners, you have the power to make order out of disorder and bring great pleasure into other people's lives, in every day living as well as on special occasions.

Why the Title?

I am the Wild Woman, the ultimate extrovert. I have no fear of walking into a room full of strangers and talking to everyone. I was a manager and leader in corporate America for over 20 years. During that time, I hired people, fired people, interviewed hundreds of people, recruited at colleges around the United States and Puerto Rico, and presided as president over many organizations. After completing a seminar on Business Etiquette in 1999, I continued researching etiquette. I have conducted 50+ etiquette seminars and workshops both for corporate and academic audiences. Now, it is time to reach a larger audience through this book. This book will start with the basics and build to more complex interactions.

Throughout this book I use "he" and "she," interchangeably as pronouns rather than using "he or she" each time when referring to people.

Chapter 1. Magical Words

Please and Thank you!

Impressing people is all about showing class. There are magical words that show class, refinement, and just plain good manners. The magical words are *please* and *thank you.* Have you noticed that these simple polite words seem to be disappearing from our vocabulary? It is not old-fashioned to be gracious. These words are so simple, yet so powerful.

Please

Whenever you ask anyone to do something for you, say "please."

Examples

Situation	DO	DON'T
Telephone call	May I *please* speak to …	Let me speak to …
Asking directions	Could you *please* tell me how to get to…?	How do I get to …
Ordering food in a restaurant	May I *please* have …	I want …
While eating	*Please* pass the salt	Pass the salt.
Shopping	Would you *please* check for this in a size 12?	Look for this in a size 12.

Thank You

After you ask someone to do something for you, say "thank you" to them after they do it. If someone pays you a compliment, all you have to say is "thank you."

Examples

Situation	DO	DON'T
Compliment on your outfit	Say *Thank you*	"Oh, this old thing? I have had it for years."
A person says to you, "You are so smart. I had no idea you knew how to do that."	Say *Thank you*	"Oh, I'm not so smart. Anyone could have done it."
A waiter serves you your meal	Say *Thank you*	Ignore the fact that your food has just been served.

I have found that women more than men are uncomfortable accepting compliments. Sure, they love being complimented, but find it awkward to respond. Perhaps it is because women don't want to appear "full of themselves" so they tend to diminish the compliment. Am I describing **you**? If so, stop it. Just respond to a compliment with a smile and a simple "thank you."

Chapter 2. The Almighty Handshake

A handshake can create a feeling of immediate friendliness or of instant irritation between two strangers. No one likes a "boneless" hand that feels like one is grasping an empty glove, nor does one appreciate a viselike grasp that feels like your hand is being broken.

When Should You Shake Someone's Hands?

According to the book *Business Etiquette for Dummies*, shaking hands is appropriate when you are: renewing an acquaintance, acknowledging, meeting or greeting someone, concluding a transaction, or leaving a business or social event.

Look at the palms of your hands. Do they look wet? Are they dry and chapped? If so, these are two features of your hands that could cause another person to instantly not like you or have misgivings about you after shaking your hand. But let's back up. Why do you want to shake someone's hand?

Shaking hands is a sign of power. Whoever extends his hand first has the power. Whether you are 13 or 80 years old, male or female, when you extend your hand for a handshake, you are demonstrating that you are confident and classy. Confidence gives you an edge in business and social relationships. Notice that I said "You are demonstrating that you are confident." In truth, you could be extremely nervous, but the handshake, if done properly, could negate your nervous appearance. No important meeting should take place or conclude without a hearty handshake.

> Tip: In both business and social situations, strive to be the first person to extend your hand for a handshake. Handshaking is an art form. When done properly, you leave a positive impression. If done improperly, you just blew it.

Tracy Laswell Williams, author and certified job and career transition coach writes in "Get a Grip: Handshaking 101" that there are 10 key factors to bear in mind during a handshake. Those factors include: timing; corresponding eye contact; facial expression and greetings; pressure; positioning; velocity; number of shakes; plane; temperature; and humidity.

Elements of a Proper Handshake

Palms should always be dry, clean, and soft. Temperature/Humidity applies Humidity affects the feel of the hand during a handshake. Have you shaken hands with a person who had wet hands? Did it feel like you were shaking hands with a fish? Wet hands are icky. Icky hands could translate to an icky person. Wait – that's not fair. Just because a person has icky hands, why would we consider the person to be icky? The answer falls into the area of "life is unfair." Remember, people form impressions of others in seconds, rightly or wrongly.

So, if you just held a glass of cold water, or if you have naturally sweaty hands, here are some ideas to help:

- Keep a handkerchief in your right pocket or nearby to dry your hand before shaking hands.
- (For naturally sweaty palms) Spray antiperspirant on your palms to keep them dry.
- Carry cold drinks in your left hand so that your right hand is dry.
- Worse case, quickly—and subtly—swipe your hands on your trousers or skirt to ensure your hand is dry before extending it.

Are Women Expected to Shake Hands?

In the old days ladies were taught that they should offer only their fingertips as the way to shake hands. That may have been fine for Scarlett O'Hara, but those days are over, especially in business. A woman who offers only her fingertips today is considered prissy and old fashioned. In today's professional environment, everyone is generally expected to shake hands, according to *Emily Post's The Etiquette Advantage in Business*. Women should shake hands with other women. It is no longer customary for a man to wait for a woman to extend her hand.

How to Shake Hands

A handshake is web to web which means placing the hand fully in one another's palm.

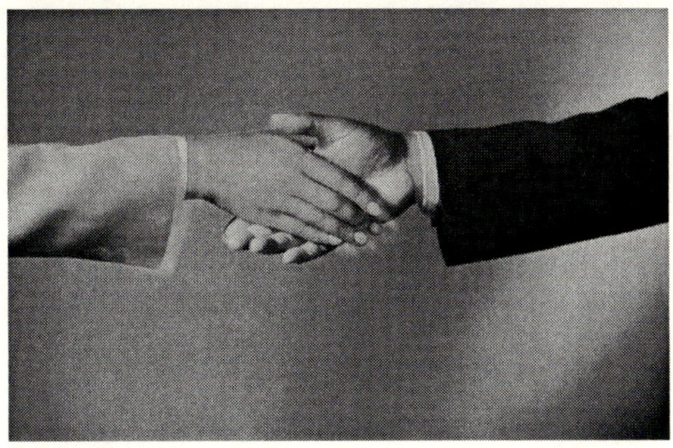

Velocity and Number of Shakes

After forming the web to web position, give a firm grip and pump the hands a couple of times in a not-too-fast manner. If your grip is too weak, you will be perceived as weak. If your grip is too strong, you will be perceived as a bully. According to Emily Post's book, your grip speaks volumes. When you shake with a medium-firm grip, you convey confidence and authority. Practice with a friend until you get it just right.

Plane

Perpendicular is the preferred position. If you extend your hand so that your palm is mostly down; you could be perceived as aggressive. Offering your handshake with your palm mostly up is considered passive.

Let Go

After two or three pumps, let go. Holding another's hand for too long could be misinterpreted as flirtation.

Clasping the outside of someone's hand with your free hand is intended to portray warmth, according to Emily Post's book. But some see the move as presumptuous, insincere, or worse, intimidating. Skip the two-handed shake in business settings.

Note: If another person holds your hand too long, don't be afraid to gently pull your hand away. Remember, you always want to be in control.

Caution – These rules apply in the United States and many other countries. There are some cultures that consider shaking hands to be rude. Prior to traveling outside of the United States, review the etiquette rules either on the web or in books like *Kiss, Bow, or Shake Hands* by Terry Morrison.

Shaking Hands with the Disabled

When you meet someone whose right arm or hand is missing or is deformed, extend your right hand even though he cannot shake hands in the normal way. The disabled person will appreciate that you have made no unnatural gesture to accommodate his disability. He will respond by offering his left hand, or by saying, "Please forgive me if I don't shake hands, but I'm very glad to meet you."

If you are disabled or are suffering an injury or illness such as arthritis and it is impossible or painful for you to shake hands, you shouldn't feel you must. Simply say, as noted above, "I'm so glad to meet you, please forgive me for not shaking hands. I have arthritis (a sprained finger or whatever the trouble may be).

Left-handed People

Always extend your right hand. It's not only customary, but you can avoid trying to attain an awkward grip.

Inappropriate Times to Shake Hands

There are times when it's actually more polite not to shake hands with someone. If the person you are meeting has his hands full, politely nod instead of forcing him to rearrange or put things down. If you have recently sneezed or coughed into your hands, rush to the bathroom before spreading your germs to others.

What if the Other Person Refuses to Shake Your Hand?

If you extend your hand to someone and are snubbed in return, simply withdraw your hand and continue your greeting, according to Emily Post's book. Remember, you want to always demonstrate professionalism and dignity even if the other person does not.

Chapter 3. Eye Contact

What are your first impressions of people who won't look you in your eyes as you are talking to them? If you are like most people, you consider those kinds of folks to be shifty, untrustworthy, and sneaky. Or in the case of children or teens, people consider them to be extremely bashful or lacking in social grace.

> Exercise
>
> Look the next five people you meet directly in the eyes as you talk with them and decide the color of their eyes.

Looking someone in the eyes shows confidence and power. But for some people, especially introverts, this is an unnatural act. If you want to show confidence, but eye contact makes you uncomfortable, what should you do? Try this. Instead of looking directly into someone's eyes, look at the area between their eyebrows. This technique is effective because they think you are making eye contact.

Chapter 4. Introductions

Generally speaking, a man is introduced to the woman: "May I present Ken Wilson. Ken, this is Darcy Brennan." When introducing people, be sure to include first and last names, even if one is the chairman of the board and the other is a junior sales representative. An introduction serves to bring people together, not reduce them to a certain rank. That means you would never introduce two people by saying, "Mr. Wilson, this is Darcy."

A young person is always introduced **to** an older person. "Dr. Harrison, I'd like you to meet my nephew, Anthony." "Uncle Charlie, this is my officemate, Gail."

A less important (I hate that term) person is always introduced **to** a more important person. This is hard to do because it is sometimes difficult to decide who is more important. Think of it as the military. "General Kornegay, I would like you to meet Sgt. Averitte."

A married woman who has retained her maiden name is introduced when she is with her husband like this: "This is Sandra Schmidt and her husband Heath Frost."

Men should stand, and most women prefer to, when being introduced to an older person. A young woman may prefer to remain seated when introduced to a slightly older man. However, she should rise when introduced to a male senior citizen much as she would stand aside and let an older man go through a door or into an elevator before she does.

When introducing two acquaintances, don't introduce one as "my friend." You may say "my brother" or "my uncle," but to pick out one person as "my friend" implies that the person you are introducing him or her to is not.

Do not speak of your spouse as "Mr. Astorino" or "Mrs. Harvey" unless you are speaking to a child. This is considered very rude to another adult. Refer to him or her as "my husband," or "my wife, Renee."

Family Introductions

When introducing members of your family, the other person is always courteously given precedence. This is not only polite, but it also makes it easier to explain your family relationship. "Pamela, my sister," or "my cousin, Paula Thornton," can only come at the **end** of an introduction. For example, a father introducing a man to his grown daughter would say, "Mr. Wilson, I'd like you to meet my daughter, Bonnie." If Bonnie is married, her last name is added: My daughter, Bonnie Muldryk."

Husbands and Wives

For formal occasions, a man introduces his wife: "Mr. Peterson, may I introduce my wife, Katie?"

To a younger man or business acquaintance, a husband would say, "Jonathan, I would like you to meet my wife," (never "the wife!") Then he adds "Katie, Jonathan Nagy."

A wife introduces her husband to friends as, "Doug" and to acquaintances as, "my husband, Doug." You may always use the forms "my husband" and "my wife" because they are proper no matter to whom you are talking.

At a Formal Dinner

Strangers sitting next to each other at the table should introduce themselves. A man says, "I am Christopher Olson" and a woman says "I am Beverly Wilder."

When a woman finds herself next to an unknown man at a dinner party, she may start talking to him without telling him her name, if she chooses. But if he introduces himself to her, she immediately may say, "I'm Marilyn Moore."

In Chapter 13, "Upscale Dining," you see that people who find themselves seated together at any table must accept the obligation of talking. To sit side-by-side without speaking is a great discourtesy to your hostess, as well as the person next to whom you are sitting. It is equally rude to devote all your time to the person on one side of you and ignore the guest on the other.

Introducing One Person to a Group

On formal occasions when many people are present, a stranger is not introduced to everyone. He should be introduced to several people and then he may talk with those near him with or without exchanging names.

It is much more effective to name those already present before naming a new arrival. The one being introduced is paying attention, of course, but one who is chatting with someone else may need to hear his own name before his attention is called to the name of the new arrival.

The well-meant practice of leading a guest on a tour around the room to make sure that she is introduced to everyone is totally unnecessary and invariably a failure. The poor stranger is hopelessly confused by too many names, and the hostess is often interrupted by the arrival of other guests.

The best practice is to leave a stranger with a nearby group, introducing her to them. Even if the hostess does not complete these introductions, the stranger will not be marooned, because in a friend's house people should *always* talk with those near them. The good hostess, however, will make every effort to see that all her guests are introduced during the course of any party of moderate size.

When Not to Introduce

At a small party it is quite all right for the hostess to introduce as many people as she can, but at a large one (such as a wedding reception) repeating never-to-be remembered names is a mistake—unless there is some good reason for doing so. For instance, if a friend wants to meet a celebrity or a person in whom he has a special interest, be sure to make the introduction.

An arriving visitor is never introduced to someone who is about to leave. If two people are engaged in conversation, a third should not approach expecting them to interrupt their talk for introductions.

What to do When Introduced

Just as you give a person who is being introduced to you your undivided attention, you look a person to whom you are being introduced in the eye and greet him or her cordially. Repeating the person's name is a technique that helps your remember the name and is a sign that you are, indeed, paying attention to the introduction. "Hello, Deb, it is a pleasure to meet you." If you don't hear a person's name or if you are not sure of what you heard, ask until you get it right.

When Incorrectly Introduced

We have all, at one time or another, been incorrectly introduced. Your name can be confused or mispronounced. It is only sensible and kind that the person being introduced correct the error immediately. If, for example, the host introduces a man to a group as "an ex-IBM manager" when he really is an ex-

Nortel manager, he should immediately explain this to the new acquaintances—and the host, if he is still there—at once.

When someone is introducing a stranger to a number of people and consistently says the name wrong, the person being introduced should correct the host as soon as he realizes it is not just a slip of the tongue. He should do so not with annoyance, but if possible, by making light of it. All he needs to say is, "I know it's confusing, but my name is Johansson, not Johnson," or "Just so you can find me in the phone book, I'm Elmer Hill, not Edward Hill."

If you are introduced by your correct name and someone immediately finds a diminutive or nickname for you, you may say, "Would you mind calling me Sharon? For some reason, I've never been called Sherry." If the other person insists on his own version, you may correct him or her one more time, and after that, ignore his discourtesy the best that you can.

Meeting Snobs or Those with No Personality

When you shake hands with someone as you introduce yourself, and the other person does not reply with his name, ask, "And your name is?" Hopefully, that will cue the person to say his name. If he doesn't, and you feel uncomfortable, say, "Nice meeting you" and move on. However, if you feel the need to have a conversation with this person, refer to Chapter 5 "Small Talk with Strangers."

Chapter 5. Small Talk with Strangers

Standing in a room full of strangers or sitting next to a stranger at a meal is awkward when no one knows how to handle small talk. Small talk allows you to learn about a person, pass time, demonstrate your social skills, and build your network.

Use the following six words to break the ice with strangers:

1. Who
2. What
3. Where
4. When
5. Why
6. How

When you ask a question, you set small talk in motion. Be careful not to sound like you are prying into someone's life. Listen to the responses and sprinkle the conversation with comments of your own that are in line with those responses. Don't give lip service as responses. Really listen and get to know the person. You never know how your paths may cross in the future.

Example:

You are at a party and only know the host. You walk up to a stranger, and shake hands.

You: "Hello, my name is Rebecca Smith."

Stranger: "Hello, Rebecca, my name is Glenn Strong."

You: "Glad to meet you Glenn. Where did you meet our host?"

Stranger: "We are neighbors. I live a few doors down."

You: "Oh, this is a lovely neighborhood. You know, I detect your accent is different than the others. Where are you from?"

Stranger: "I am from Chicago."

You: "What brought you to North Carolina?"

Get the idea? None of the questions are yes/no, because those are closed questions that do not extend a conversation. No need to cling to that person for the rest of the evening. After a few minutes, end the conversation with, "Nice talking to you, Glenn" and move along to someone else. Make it a point to meet as many people as possible using this small talk method. You will appear confident and gracious.

Chapter 6. Thank You Notes

Sure, it is polite to say "Thank You," but there are certain events where a thank you note is mandatory to show good manners. Those events are:

- For wedding presents
- After dinner at your boss's home
- After receiving a present by mail
- After a weekend visit
- After receiving a gift when you are sick
- For letters of condolence
- After being the guest of honor at a party

The sooner you write a thank-you note, the better. If you put off writing, your appreciation might sound false. Ideally, send your thank-you note within one week. Using your engraved stationery is really a classy touch.

Sending a thank-you note after a dinner party is not mandatory, but I strongly suggest sending one. It will be a pleasant surprise and give the host a positive impression about you.

Printed Thank-You Notes

Printed thank-you cards that you purchase at a card shop and e-cards suffice as thank-you notes, but they don't take the place of a personal message. If you do send a card or e-card, be sure to include a line or two of your own.

Chapter 7. Name Tags

Name tags tell the world who you are. They are a good visual aid for people who have trouble remembering names at business and social functions. There are two types of name tags. The more familiar name tag is the kind you affix to your clothing. The second type is the one attached to a lanyard that hangs around your neck.

Placement

The horizontal placement of the name tag that you affix to your clothes is a function of the context in which you wear it. Name tags will be easily visible in the line of sight of your handshake. That means you should wear your name tag on your right. The person shaking your hand can look directly up your arm to your eyes, catching your name along the way.

On the other hand, Scott Ginsberg, author of "The Seven Deadly Sins of Ineffective Nametags" writes that for mobile and populated events such as trade shows, expos and conventions, it may be more effective to wear your name tag on your left side. This allows people who approach in your opposite direction to see your name tag with significant ease, because we traditionally walk on the right side of the aisle or hallway.

While lanyard or necklace style name tags are desirable because they reduce clothing damage, they often get accidentally turned around or become tangled at some point. People approaching you can't read your name or your company name, and there go the network opportunities. Someone who doesn't know your name and sees your turned around name tag might shrug his shoulders, turn away and find another person to talk to. The answer is to have the information on both sides.

Make sure your name tag does not hang too low. It will be impossible for other people to read it when you sit down, or cross your arms.

Chapter 8. Netiquette — e-mail Etiquette in the World of Business

Thanks to technology, many people use e-mail as their primary form of communication. Unfortunately, etiquette seems to have disappeared as people fire off note after note without regard to consideration of the recipients. You are judged for your e-mails the same way you are judged in polite society.

Just as business conversations should be concise and to the point, the same applies to e-mails. Your business correspondence should not, if possible, exceed one viewable page on the computer. That's because most readers do not read more than the first few lines of an e-mail. When responding to questions, answer all questions as thoroughly as possible in order to avoid further e-mails asking for further information about the same questions.

Proper spelling, grammar, and punctuation are mandatory. This is important because improper spelling, grammar, and punctuation give your company a bad impression and may convey the wrong message. E-mails with incorrect punctuation are difficult to read and can sometimes alter the meaning of the note. Proofread your e-mails before you send them. A lot of people don't bother to read an e-mail before they send it out. Reading your e-mail through the eyes of the recipient will help you send a more effective message and avoid misunderstandings and inappropriate comments.

For critical e-mails read the e-mail backwards. It is hard to find your own mistakes. If you read the last sentence first and move backwards in the e-mail, you will be more likely to find any errors.

Respond Swiftly

Although in-boxes fill up fast, scan your messages in two places in order to set priority for responses: (1) Sender and (2) Subject. Reply to "important" people as soon as possible. Important people can be your prime customers, your boss, or someone you are trying to impress. Review the subject line to assess how critical the message is. People misuse the "urgent" option thinking that their notes will get a higher priority. You should be the judge on whether or not an e-mail is urgent in deciding how fast to reply.

Consider Your Reader

Do not send unnecessary attachments. They bog down the system, especially for users on dial-up.

Do not write in CAPITALS. It is called "screaming" and is an annoyance.

Be careful with "Reply to All." You could be filling up in-boxes with notes that need to be sent only to the originator.

Abbreviations and emoticons are popular in casual e-mails. Avoid overusing them in business. "r u in agreement?" is cute and pithy, but has no place in an e-mail to executives.

Do not forward chain letters. We can safely say that all of them are hoaxes. Just delete the letters as soon as you receive them, especially if they end with "Don't break this chain." More importantly, they are an annoyance to your recipient.

Do not request delivery and read receipts. This may annoy your recipient before she has even read your message. Besides, it usually does not work anyway since the recipient could have blocked that function, or her software might not support it, so what is the use of using it? If you want to know whether an e-mail was received it is better to ask the recipient to let you know if it was received.

Avoid over-using Urgent and Important. Those two features become the "boy who cried wolf." If your recipients get too many notes from you that turn out to be non-urgent and non-important, they will ignore your notes or make them a low priority.

Avoid long sentences. Readers will stop reading your e-mail. Capture your thoughts in your e-mail, review it, and cut both the length of the e-mail and the length of your sentences.

Never, NEVER send or forward e-mails containing offensive, racist or obscene remarks. This is the epitome of crude behavior and reflects poorly on you.

Use cc: sparingly. Only include those who have an intense interest in your e-mail. When you mention any third party's name, be sure to cc: that person as well. However, if you receive an e-mail and that third party wasn't cc:'d ask the sender to please resend the e-mail and include that person.

Before responding to e-mail, look to see if anyone was cc:'d. If so, hit "Reply All" so that everyone who has an interest in the outcome stays in the loop. However, if your reply is controversial and shouldn't be aired to the cc: list, write a separate e-mail to the cc: list indicating you have responded with questions and will cc: them when the final decision is reached.

Chapter 9. Telephone Etiquette

Leaving Messages

Don't you just hate it when someone leaves you a telephone message and doesn't leave a callback number, or says his name so fast, you can't understand it? What are your thoughts about that person? In business it could mean a missed opportunity.

When you leave a telephone message, pause between your first and last name, especially if you have a complicated name. Spell your name to make it easier for the recipient to be clear about your name.

Say your telephone number slowly at the beginning and end of your message. Many people may not have a pen or pencil handy. By repeating your number, you do the recipient a favor by giving him an opportunity to write your number. Cell phones capture telephone numbers, so your recipient can just do a callback on your number, but what if you want your recipient to call you at another number? Make a habit to repeat your telephone number. When you give your telephone number, pause between the area code, prefix, and last four numbers. That way, your recipient won't have to replay your message to capture your telephone number.

Placing a Telephone Call

Unless you are making calls to good friends who automatically recognize your voice, ask, "Is Pat there?" and immediately identify yourself: "This is Ann Jones." This sets the tone for you as being polite. Never assume the person on the other end knows who you are.

Long-Winded Callers

Whoever places the call should be the one to offer to end the call. However, some people love to talk on the telephone and have plenty of time to do so. If you're caught in a conversation that seems unending, you'll have to take the initiative. *Amy Vanderbilt Complete Book of Etiquette* suggests you wait until the person pauses for a breath and say, "Oh, dear! I've just noticed the time. I'm late for an appointment." You don't have to be rude, but you may have to be emphatic.

Cell Phones and Pagers

Cell phones and pagers offer a tremendous amount of flexibility that people enjoy every day. With this technology come rules to ensure that you, as a user, should follow to avoid annoying others and appearing unprofessional.

Shut off your cell phone and pager (or put them on vibrate) at the movies, the theater, and the opera. Paying customers are at these events to enjoy themselves and get extremely annoyed when a cell phone or pager goes off. This situation is even worse at a live performance. Unless there are exceptions, turn off your cell phone and pager in business meetings.

Be considerate of others when using a cell phone in a public place. Don't cross the personal space boundary. Find an isolated spot so others don't need to hear your conversation.

For safety's sake, act responsibly when walking or driving while on a cell phone. Some states have outlawed using your cell phone while driving. While you are focusing on your call, you diminish your attention toward driving and walking.

Don't shout into the telephone. Keep your conversation private.

Respect the rules of establishments and airlines if asked to refrain from using cell phones and pagers.

Speakerphones

For business calls, a speakerphone is a handy tool that allows multiple people to sit in one room and hear the call. The call leader should identify all persons in the room and have all participants on the call identify themselves.

Do not chew gum or eat while on a call. Everyone on the all can hear this disruptive noise. Make sure your speakerphone is on mute if you have to eat. Some business continues to get done while on speakerphone calls. This usually means that participants type while listening to the call. Once again, make sure you have your speakerphone on mute while you are typing. Verify that music does not play while your speakerphone is on mute.

Think of your personal pet peeves while on speakerphone calls.

Whatever annoys you, annoys others. Be sensitive to those on the call. Remember, you are being judged even if people can't see you.

And for goodness sakes, make sure your speakerphone is on mute if you are talking to your co-workers and you say disparaging things about someone else on the call. Not cool. Better yet, don't say disparaging things at all!

Office Telephones

Avoid lengthy personal phone calls in the office. Sometimes you can't avoid a personal call, but long chatty conversations are not only out of place, but can get you in trouble. Your chatter annoys other people in the office or cubicles who cannot help overhearing and interrupts the routine of office procedure.

Electronic Answering Systems

Businesses have cut back administrative positions and installed computerized systems that answer calls electronically. Sometimes, the most annoying aspect of these systems is having to listen to a menu of options to reach a department or person, only to get yourself into a loop or lost trying to make your call. You can press "0" to reach a live person. Do not take out your annoyance on the person who answers. He has nothing to do with the installation of the system. Remember to be professional because if anyone overhears your conversation, you want to make sure you don't come off as a hothead.

Chapter 10. Business Cards

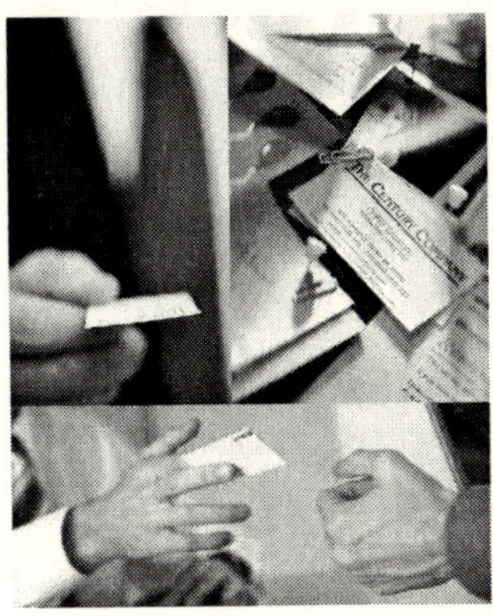

Business cards are a personal reflection of you. Be sure your business cards are crisp (not wrinkled), and have nothing handwritten or scratched out on them.

Proper protocol in business and social situations usually includes business card exchange. A person of higher rank may offer their card to you. Accept the card and look at it for a few seconds. If appropriate, make a positive comment about the card, such as the logo, the design, quality of the paper or embossing.

When presenting your card, present it properly: face up so that the writing can be read.

For business meetings, give out your cards at the beginning of a meeting. Ideally, present your cards to individuals at the meetings. Do not pass them around a conference room table. There are two reasons for this giving out your cards at the beginning of a meeting -- doing it up front ensures you won't be forgotten, and having the cards of others in front of you will help you remember the names of the people you are meeting with. Consider placing other's cards in front of you for the duration of the meeting.

Sherri Ferris, President and CEO of Protocol Professionals, Inc. offers the following business card suggestions:

- Never run out of business cards or BE WITHOUT a business card unless you are in the shower.
- Use sufficiently large print so that the information can be read easily. Your name should be the largest print on the card.
- If one person asks for a business card, the other should offer his/hers in return.

- Choose high quality paper and ink with thermography or engraving so that the printing is raised.

- Never pass out business cards like you are "dealing cards." Keep them in a business card case and present them so that the recipient can read them right side up. It is polite to comment on the card before putting it away rather than immediately stashing it in a pocket without looking at it.

- In Asian cultures, use two hands to give and receive cards, and place your counterpart's card on the tabletop during a business meeting. In cultures such as Japan, the exchange of business cards is a very formal and respectful process, taking a great deal of time.

- If traveling abroad, have your cards printed on one side in the language of the country you are visiting.

- Writing notes about the person who gave you a card is very helpful e.g. the date you met them, the occasion, and any follow-up. But don't do this in the presence of that individual, especially when you are with individuals from other countries.

- When networking, keep your business card case handy in an easily accessible pocket. It's too difficult to rummage for cards at a stand-up reception while you are balancing a plate and beverage glass!

Chapter 11. Mama Always Said

Did your mama (or dad, grandmother, etc.) teach you basic etiquette while your were growing up? Does it annoy you to see that those things you were taught are being ignored today? Let's review some of those basic teachings. Each one speaks for itself.

1. If you want to be treated with respect, treat everyone you meet with respect. This is the similar to: Do unto others as you would have others do unto you.
2. If you want to be treated like a lady, act like one.
3. Stay sober.
4. Respect your elders.
5. Say please and thank you (See Chapter 1.)
6. Chew with your mouth closed.
7. Gentlemen should offer their seats and open the door for ladies. (This one could be controversial because of issues of equality, but most of the women I know enjoy this treatment.)
8. Cover your mouth when you sneeze. (It helps to always carry tissue or a handkerchief.)
9. Never "pop" your chewing gum in the presence of others.
10. The way you treat a waitperson is the way you treat others. Remember, you are being judged at all times. If you are snippy and rude to your waitperson, observers will see unpleasant insights into your personality.

Chapter 12. Miscellaneous Business Etiquette

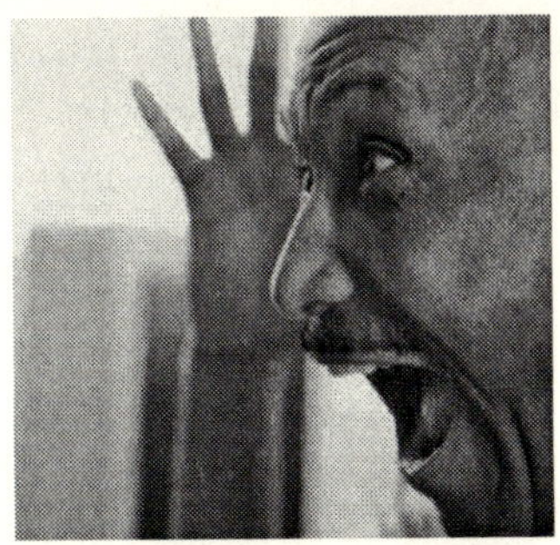

I asked some business associates to provide me with their top business etiquette pet peeves. If you have a staff of people who deal with customers, or if you have face to face dealings with customers, read on.

1. Sales people should give priority to the store customer rather than the person on the phone. For example, you approach a retail counter and the clerk greets you, starts to take care of you, and then answers the telephone and helps the caller instead of you. This behavior causes you, the in-store customer, to feel slighted. The clerk can answer the telephone, but should put the caller on hold until he finishes with the in store customer.

2. At a grocery store, be sure you have less than 12 items (or whatever the store sets as a limit) before getting into the Express Line. Everyone's time is valuable. The people in line with the correct number of items deserve to be respected for following the rules.

3. Customer representatives and support should treat customers with respect and not treat them like idiots for asking questions. If the customer knew the answer, she wouldn't be calling. These representatives reflect badly on the company.

4. Customer representatives should speak slowly when giving directions to the caller. If the caller is writing the information, it doesn't help if the representative speeds through the instructions.

5. Some department store clerks act as if they are annoyed when a customer wants to make a purchase. They don't seem to realize that the customer is the one who is paying their salary.

6. Please find a delicate way to tell a man that his fly is open or he has a goober in his nose. Pull him to the side and out of earshot of others and quietly say something like, "You might want to check your pants," or "You might want to check your nose." Tell a woman immediately that she has lipstick on her teeth.

7. When someone says "Thank you," respond with "You're welcome." Avoid "No problem" or "You bet." It's the polite thing to do.
8. Learn to speak correct English, PLEASE. "Like, you know, like," becomes annoying because the speaker is not offering a complete sentence. To quote the esteemed Lem Kornegay "Grammar is a reflection of one's mind and soul."

Chapter 13. Upscale Dining

People are always watching you. Some know the rules of proper dining etiquette and watch you to see if you are demonstrating that you know these rules. Surprise everyone by practicing the dining rules that you will learn in this chapter. Practice as often as possible. You want to do the right thing without having to give it much thought.

Making a Reservation

Let's assume you are going to a fine restaurant. It could be for your prom, to celebrate a special occasion, to treat yourself because you deserve it, or interviewing for a job over lunch or dinner.

Unless you are someone's guest, make reservations. Call the restaurant a week or two ahead of the date of your meal. Advise the person taking your reservation of the following information:

- Your name
- Number of people in your party
- Time you would like to be seated

Some restaurants want the gentlemen to wear jackets. Others do not allow sneakers or athletic wear. Always inquire beforehand about its rules on attire. Verify that the restaurant has the correct information about your reservation and remember to say thank you before hanging up.

The Day or Evening of the Reservation

Valet Service

Some restaurants have a valet located in front of the restaurant. A valet is a service a restaurant offers to allow its guests to avoid parking problems. The valet's service is to take your car, park it, and return it to you as you leave the restaurant.

After you pull into the valet area, leave your keys in the car and step out of the car. The valet will give you the ticket that you need to retrieve your car later. There is no need to tip the valet until you leave the restaurant.

At the Restaurant

After you enter the restaurant, walk to the reservation desk. Say hello, give your name and reservation time.

Example – Hello, my name is Sharon Hill. I have reservation for four at 7:30, please.

The person will check the book to find your reservation and see that you and your party get seated. Men should make sure all the women are seated before they sit. Thank the person who seats you after you are seated. In upscale restaurants the captain or waitperson will unfold your napkin and place it on your lap. If this doesn't happen, feel free to place your napkin on your lap yourself.

If water is on the table as you are seated, it is appropriate to sip your water after everyone is seated and after you have placed your napkin on your lap. Do not help yourself to the bread basket and other communal foods until your host has indicated you may do so. If you pick up the bread basket, hold the basket and offer to the person to your left, then serve yourself, and then pass the basket to the person on your right. (The same applies to butter, salad dressings, and other condiments that are passed.)

Posture at the Table

Elbows, elbows, if you're able – keep your elbows off the table! Proper posture at the table is very important. Sit up straight (but not stiffly) with your arms held near your body. You should neither lean on the back of the chair nor bend forward to place the elbows on the table. Elbows may rest gently on the edge if the table between courses, but not while you are eating. Don't take up more elbow room than you need while eating; be considerate of your neighbors. You should not push your chair back and cross your legs until the meal is completely finished. Crossing your legs during the meal can cause you to slouch, and looks too casual.

It is all right to rest your wrists on the edge of the table or place your hands in your lap.

Glasses, Plates, Flatware

So many glasses, so many forks. What are you supposed to do with all that stuff? You see forks on your left. You see a knife and spoons on your right. You may even see smaller forks and spoons above your plate. Wine, water glasses, and coffee cups are all around the table. Let's discuss everything in detail.

The simple rule to follow is to begin with the silverware on the outside of the place setting and work your way in toward your plate with each course. The forks generally line up for three courses: salad, entrée, and dessert. The same applies to the spoons on the right. The outer spoon is the soup spoon. Moving to the left (and towards your plate) is the teaspoon. The knife is between the teaspoon and your plate. The knife is used for cutting your food as you eat. You have a separate knife to butter your bread. Remember, we are discussing upscale restaurants. If the restaurant does not have butter knives, use your regular knife. The salad fork and knife are those closest to the plate, but if the entrée and the salad are served at the same time, go ahead and use the entrée fork for both.

More about Knives

The dinner knife is the largest knife by your plate. The dinner knife may also be used to cut your salad if the leaves are too large to fit into your mouth. The steak knife, as well as the fish knife, if you have either of these, will be located to the right of the dinner knife. The steak knife has a serrated edge and a pointed tip, whereas the fish knife has an unusual shape and a smooth edge.

Use either your dinner knife or steak knife to push small pieces of food such as peas or corn onto your fork. Choose the one that is most natural and comfortable for you.

Put your knife across the top of your plate when you are eating, blade facing toward you.

More about Spoons

There are two different-sized soup spoons, a large one for a thick soup that will be served in a bowl, and a smaller one if you are having consommé. Your dessert spoon has a longer and narrower bowl than the other spoons. After eating your dessert, place your dessert spoon on your dessert plate.

You may have received an iced tea spoon if you order iced tea. Similarly, a demitasse spoon will probably be served with your espresso, if you order one. It is a tiny spoon made expressly for stirring espresso. Rest it on the saucer when you are finished.

Bread and Butter Plate

Located above the forks is the bread and butter plate with a small knife. That small knife is your butter knife to be used to cut your bread. Dessert spoons and forks are usually brought in with the dessert, but often the dessert silver is place above the dinner plate.

You will see water, beverage, wine glasses and coffee cup/saucer above the spoons and knife. Your plate is between the silverware. Some restaurants put a smaller plate on top of your plate. Others may place the soup bowl on top of your plate. Don't be worried about having extra plates or bowls. Your waitperson will remove them before or when you receive your food.

More on Plates

Other plates include the dinner/luncheon plate, the service plate, the dessert plate, and the cup and saucer. The dinner/luncheon plate is the largest plate in the setting and is found in the middle of the place setting. Dinner plates are larger than luncheon plates, and the one in your place setting is determined by whether you are eating dinner or lunch. Your place setting will have one or the other, not both.

The service plate often serves as a salad or luncheon plate as well. You will most often find the service plate on top of your dinner plate. It is used to hold appetizers and soup bowls and is removed after these courses. If appetizers and soup aren't included in the meal, the waitperson will remove the service plate before the entrée is served.

Upon completion of the entrée, the waitperson removes the dinner plate and replaces it with the dessert plate. The plate is placed in the center of the place setting plate. Like the dinner plate, the dessert plate remains in the center of the place setting when you are finished.

Salad Plate

You will find your salad plate in one of two places, either to the left of your napkin or on top of your dinner plate in the middle of the place setting. The salad plate is smaller than the dinner plate but larger than the bread and butter plate. To save space at large pre-set banquet tables you will often find your salad plate above your forks. If you are dining in a restaurant and your salad plate is on top of your dinner plate you may place the salad plate to the left of the dinner plate if you want to eat your salad with or after your entrée.

B M W

Have you ever sat at a round elegant table and struggled trying to figure out which goblet of water or iced tea is yours? Here is a simple tip that makes it easy to remember.

Your Bread plate is always on your left. Your Meal plate is always in the center. Your Water or Wine glass (or anything Wet) is always on your right. Remembering this simple idea will prevent you from taking the wrong bread plate or drinking from your dining neighbor's water goblet. I know of an upcoming junior executive whose career got stalemated because he took a senior executive's bread plate. These rules can have serious consequences if not practiced properly.

If you get a piece of soiled silverware, simply ask the waitperson for a clean utensil. If you drop a piece of silverware, pick it up if you can reach it, and ask the waitperson for a clean one. If it is out of reach, let the waitperson know you dropped it.

Wine Steward

If you and your party appreciate fine wine, or even if you don't know the difference between a rose' and a chardonnay, the wine steward (also called a sommelier pronounced se-mel-'ya with a long A) can assist you. The wine steward is an expert who can provide suggestions for wine to accompany your meal. Be careful. A restaurant that employs a wine steward doesn't usually stock grocery store varieties. One bottle of wine could cost as much as a compact car. If money is no object and you want to enjoy a fine wine with your meal, let your wine steward suggest an appropriate one.

Here is the process. The wine steward (or if there is none, the captain or waitperson), will show you the wine list. You may pass the decision to someone at the table more knowledgeable about wines. If no one at the table knows a thing about wine, you may ask the wine steward to recommend a suitable wine. It is perfectly acceptable for you to suggest a modestly priced wine.

After the wine is selected, the wine steward shows you the bottle before uncorking it. This is to allow you to verify it is the wine you ordered. After opening the bottle, the wine steward may give you the cork so that you can feel that it is strong; you may sniff the cork to be sure it is free from any musty smell. The wine steward then pours a small amount of wine into your wine glass. You should taste the wine and may smell its bouquet to be sure it's good. Another reason for pouring the wine first into your glass is so that you will receive any bits of cork that may have been floating at the top of the bottle. If you like the wine, give the okay to the wine steward. During the meal the waitperson refills the wine glasses. Glasses are filled only half-way. Guests should not have to pour the wine themselves.

Tipping the Wine Steward

Tip the wine steward 15 to 20 percent of the wine bill if he helped you make the wine selection, paid attention to your budget request and made sure you and your guests had timely refills. Tip between 10 and15 percent if he only took your order and poured your first glass of wine. How much you give depends on the number of bottles as well as the price of the wine. The wine steward is paid in cash. He will make himself available when he sees you are getting ready to leave or may ask you if you want more wine when he sees you have finished your wine. If you don't wish to order anymore, you may thank him and give him his tip at that time rather than waiting until you depart.

If your waitperson is the person handling the wine responsibility, there is no special tip for his wine service.

What about Non-wine Drinkers?

If the wine steward comes to your table or if your waitperson presents a wine list to you, politely say, "No, thank you." If you are at a banquet where a waitperson is automatically pouring wine into everyone's glass, just place two fingers on the rim of your glass (before they pour, of course) and say, "No, thank you." DO NOT TURN YOUR WINE GLASS UPSIDE DOWN. The only drink item turned upside down is a coffee cup. This indicates to the waitperson that you will not be having coffee or tea.

White Wine or Red Wine?

You may order wine from the wine steward after the choices for the meal have been made. If there is no wine steward, order from your waitperson. A white wine is a good choice when you order chicken or fish. It is customary to choose a red wine when ordering steaks or other red meat.. It is acceptable to order a bottle of each. A vin rose` (pink wine) is a compromise for all and goes well with many entrees.

Most restaurants offer wine by the glass, an ideal solution when two people dining together want different wines or think one bottle is too much wine. If you have a definite preference for red or white wine (e.g. you drink burgundy with your fish), it is perfectly acceptable to order whatever pleases you with any meal. Do not be intimidated by the wine police!

Drinking from Stemware

Wine and champagne glasses with long stems should be held by the stem. This keeps the heat of the hand from warming the beverage. Heavy water goblets or glasses with shorter stems must be held by the bowl of the glass to keep the glass balanced. Some prefer to hold glasses of red wine or brandy by the bowl of the glass because the heat of the hand warms the wine and enhances the flavor.

Ordering the Meal

If you enjoy the Victorian structure of having the gentleman order for the lady, go for it. The lady tells the gentleman what she'll have and he tells the waitperson. I suggest making it easy for the waitperson by having each person order directly. The waitperson will start with the lady and go around the table.

If you see something on the menu, and you have no idea what it is, ask the waitperson. There is nothing to be embarrassed about. Escargot may sound fancy, but you may not be happy with snails. Calamari sounds exotic, but squid may cause you to spit your food into your napkin. (By the way, calamari tastes like breaded mushrooms to me, so don't be afraid to try it.)

In order to get your waitperson's attention, say, "Excuse me" when he is nearby, wave your hand slightly when he is looking at you, or ask a nearby employee to notify him that you request his assistance. To show that you are ready to order, close your menu and place it on the table.

Order your appetizer, salad, soup and entrée at the same time. Order dessert after everyone has finished their entrees. The waitperson will bring you a separate dessert menu, or wheel a dessert cart to your table.

When (and How) Do We Eat?

When you are seated at a table of six people, it is courteous to wait until everyone has been served before you begin eating. At a larger table, you may begin to eat after three or four people have been served. If you are one of the first few to be served, eat slowly and let others catch up. Do not put too much food into your mouth and do not talk with your mouth full. Never chew with your mouth open or make loud noises when you eat. When cutting food (meat, salad, etc.) cut enough for two or three mouthfuls and eat those before cutting more. Don't cut your whole steak, salmon steak, or leg of lamb all at once. Place your used teabag beside your cup on your saucer. If food falls off of your plate onto the table, you may pick it up with a piece of your silverware and place it on the edge of your plate.

Eating Bread

Bread should always be broken into moderate-sized pieces with the fingers before being eaten. To butter it, hold a piece on the edge of the bread-and-butter plate and with the butter knife spread enough butter on it for a mouthful or two at a time. Remember, if there is no butter knife, use whatever knife is available.

Bread should never be held on the palm of your hand and buttered with the hand held in the air. To serve yourself from a butter dish, use the butter knife, not your own, unless your knife is clean and there is no butter knife. Butter should be taken when passed, and placed onto your bread plate, never directly onto your bread.

Pass the Salt

Salt and pepper are always passed together, even if someone asks only for the salt. They are considered "married" in proper dining etiquette.

Eating Soup

Soup may be served in a cup or in a wide soup plate. Sip from the side of the spoon without inserting the whole bowl of the spoon into your mouth. Soup in a cup may be sipped with a spoon until it has cooled a bit. Then, you can drink it from the cup if you like. Use your spoon to eat any vegetables or meat at the bottom of the cup. When you near the bottom of a cup or a plate of soup, tip the dish away from you to eat the last few spoonfuls. You may tip the spoon either toward you or away from you, but I strongly recommend you dip your spoon away from yourself to fill it with soup. Do this to prevent spilling soup on yourself. After you have finished, rest the spoon on the saucer or plate under the bowl. If the soup plate is a large one and the plate beneath it is small, rest the spoon in the empty soup plate.

When large crackers are served with soup, eat them separately. Do not break them up and sprinkle them into your soup. Messy, messy.

One final word on eating soup. Sip soup, don't slurp it. Slurping is noisy and considered uncouth (unless you are in Japan where it is considered a compliment to the cook).

Used Silverware

Once silverware is picked up from the table, it never touches the table again because it might dirty the tablecloth. Place it on the outer rim of the plate between bites, but never rest half on the plate and half on the table. At the end of each course, a utensil must not be left in any dish that is not flat, such as the shrimp cocktail dish, a teacup or a parfait glass. All these items are usually presented with a plate underneath the bowl or cup, on which the utensil must be placed after use. A soup bowl is flat and acceptable to leave a soup spoon.

Resting at the Table

When you are resting, not using the utensils at the table, but you are not finished eating, place your fork tines down over the knife on the plate. This is a signal to the waitperson not to remove your plate. When you are not eating, keep your hands in your lap. Don't fidget.

Napkins Can Talk?

A napkin is not a bib, nor is it a handkerchief. Never use your napkin as a handkerchief unless it is an absolute emergency, especially if the napkin is made of cloth. Women should try not to get lipstick on cloth napkins. Use your napkin to blot, not wipe, your mouth. If you spill on the tablecloth, wipe up the spill with your napkin, and tell your waitperson so she can take whatever action is necessary to prevent a stain.

Napkins don't actually speak, but you can use your napkin to "talk" to your waitperson. What if you need to use the restroom or leave the room to make a telephone call? (I just know you would never use your cell phone at the table, right?) Place your napkin in your chair as an indication to your waitperson that you will be returning and not to take your plate. You may place the napkin on the seat, on the arm, or back of your chair.

Note: There is one exception to this rule. If your napkin is yucky and disgusting because you have soiled it with food or sauce, fold it up to hide the stains and place it to the left of your plate. A dirty napkin could soil the chair or stain your clothing if you sit on it by mistake when you return. Remember to apologize for having to leave the table.

If your napkin falls on the floor and is within easy reach, retrieve it. If you are unable to retrieve the napkin without drawing attention to yourself, ask your waitperson for another one.

When you have finished your meal, place your napkin partly folded, never crumpled, at the left of your plate. Even a paper napkin should never be crushed and tossed into your plate. When your waitperson sees your napkin on the left side of your plate, she knows she has your permission to remove your plate. Per the note above, you may return to the table to find your plate has been removed if the waitperson sees your napkin on the left side of your plate. You have been warned.

In addition to your napkin, another way to indicate that you are finished with the meal is to place your knife and fork at the 4:00 position on your plate. Do not push your plate away or otherwise rearrange your dishes from their position when you are finished.

Meal Courses

Upscale restaurants serve courses in this order:

1. Aperitif
2. Appetizer
3. Soup
4. Salad
5. Sorbet Intermezzo
6. Entrée
7. Dessert
8. Coffee

Aperitif

An aperitif is usually an alcoholic drink taken before a meal. Aperitifs include *Lillet, Dubonnet, Campari, Cinzano,* dry or sweet vermouths and sherry. They may be served either in a small old-fashioned glass with ice, or chilled, or at room temperature in a small aperitif glass. An aperitif can also be cheese and fruit that are offered before the meal.

Sorbet Intermezzo

The dictionary describes an intermezzo as “a brief interlude or diversion.” In dining a sorbet intermezzo is an interlude between the appetizer and entrée to cleanse your palate, so that you can have full enjoyment of your entrée. Sorbet is French for sherbet. Sorbet is served with a small chilled spoon. If the sorbet is served on ice, do not eat the ice.

Tipping at a Restaurant

You will need money to tip various service people at the restaurant. Here is a guide.

Restaurants/Bars	
Waiter/Waitress	15% of bill (excluding tax) for adequate service; 20% for very good service; no less than 10% for poor service
Headwaiter/captain	Often gets a cut of table server's tip; so tip your server extra to reward captain, or tip captain separately
Sommelier, or wine steward	15% of cost of the bottle
Bartender	15% to 20% of the bar tab, with a minimum of 50 cents per soft drink, $1 per alcoholic drink
Coatroom attendant	$1 per coat
Parking valet or garage attendant	$2 to bring car to you
Washroom attendant	50 cents to $1

CNN/Money 2005

Buffet Etiquette

The beauty of a buffet is that it allows you to see all the dining choices and put food onto your plate without having to be dependent on your waitperson. You are still being watched and should be aware of buffet etiquette to avoid making a bad impression. Basically, remember the following simple rules:

- Use a new plate each time you return to the buffer line. Leave your used plate on your table. Your waitperson will remove it from table.
- Do not cut in line
- Do not eat as you move through the buffet line
- Always use utensils to place food on your plate
- Be considerate of those behind you in line. For example, don't pick each piece of lettuce individually for your salad and take forever to build your salad plate.
- Do not overload your plate. It makes you look gluttonous. Take smaller portions and return to the buffet line with your clean plate.
- Keep your silverware at the table. Your waitperson will remove your dirty plate, and will place your silverware on the table your placemat.
- Do not ask for a to-go container. Buffets do not allow food to be taken out. (I saw some children carrying cookies out of a buffet at a Las Vegas buffet. A buffet employee confiscated the cookies before the children could walk out.). There is a fixed price for the buffet and individuals must consume the food on the premises.
- Tip your waitperson 10 percent of your bill (not including tax). Even though you are getting your food yourself from the buffet, your waitperson gets your drinks and condiments at upscale buffets. Some are available to get additional portions of buffet items for you. Note: When using discount coupons, your tip is 10% of the cost of the meal prior to deducting the coupon.

Foods You Can Eat With Your Fingers

Artichokes. To eat it, pull a leaf off, dip it, scrape the flesh from the base of the leaf with your top teeth, and discard the leaf on the plate provided for that purpose. Continue eating the leaves until the prickly "choke" is revealed. Switch to fork and knife, first to remove the choke, then to eat the heart and base.

Asparagus. Asparagus may be eaten with the fingers as long as it is not covered with sauce or too mushy to pick up easily. Of course, it is also fine to use a fork and knife to eat asparagus.

Bacon. When bacon is cooked until it is crisp, and there is no danger of getting your fingers wet with grease, it is okay to pick it up to eat it. Trying to cut a crisp piece of bacon and pick it up with a fork could be a chore.

Cookies. When a dessert is garnished with a cookie, pick it up and eat it with your fingers unless it has fallen so far into the chocolate sauce that there isn't a clean corner by which to pick it up.

Hors d'Oeuvres, Canapes, Crudités. Almost everything that is served at a cocktail party is intended to be eaten with the fingers. This includes olives, pickles, nuts, deviled eggs, and chips. Crudités (pronounced kru-di-`ta with a long A) are pieces of raw vegetables (as carrots or celery) served as an hors d'oeuvre often with a dip.

Small fruits and berries on the stem. Strawberries with the hulls on, cherries with stems, or grapes in bunches are okay to eat with fingers. Otherwise, as with all berries, the utensil of choice is a spoon. When eating a cluster of grapes, tear a portion from the whole, rather than plucking off single grapes.

Removing Unwanted Food from the Mouth

The general rule for removing food from your mouth is that is should go out the same way it went in. Therefore, olive pits can be delicately dropped onto an open palm before putting then onto your plate, and a piece of bone discovered in a bite of chicken should be returned to the plate by way of the fork. Fish is an exception to the rule. It is fine to remove the tiny bones with your fingers, because they would be difficult to drop from your mouth onto the fork. And, of course, if what you have to spit out will be grossly ugly, such as an extremely fatty piece of meat that you simply can't bring yourself to swallow, spit it into your napkin, so that you can keep it out of sight.

If your food is too hot to eat, try taking a drink of water or another cold beverage instead of removing the food from your mouth. If you take a bite of something you don't like (but are not allergic to) swallow it as quickly as possible. However, if you take a bite of something that is spoiled, by all means remove it as described. To remove food stuck in your teeth, excuse yourself and remove it in the restroom. The bottom line is to use whatever method will draw the least attention to you.

What if You Have to Sneeze?

If you have to sneeze, turn your head away from the table and away from all others, if possible, and put your handkerchief or hand over your mouth and nose when you sneeze. If you must blow your nose, excuse yourself from the table. If you cannot be excused, turn your head away and do it quickly and quietly.

Ewwwww. He has a Piece of Broccoli Caught in His Teeth.

If someone else has food stuck in his teeth, you should tell him quietly and discretely. If you are on the receiving end of such a message, thank the person for telling you, excuse yourself, and go to the restroom to remove the food from your teeth, or use your napkin to remove it if it is on your face. You should never use toothpicks at the table, or try to remove food from your teeth with your tongue or fingers.

If your wear braces, keep them clean and watch what you eat so you don't have food caught in them. Women should try to keep lipstick off their braces.

Left-Handers

If you or someone you are dining with is left-handed, it is best for the left-handed person to sit at the left end of the table or at the head of the table. This arrangement helps ensure that everyone has adequate elbow-room to eat comfortably.

Shrimp Cocktail

If shrimp is in the shell, carefully remove the shell by holding the legs in your fingers and peeling the shell around and off. Hold the shrimp by the tail and dip it in the sauce. It is also acceptable to use your fork, spear a shrimp, dip it into the sauce and eat it. This is the method you may prefer when the shrimp has already been cleaned and shelled before serving. Shells are to be left in the cocktail bowl or on your bread and butter plate.

Spaghetti

Twirling spaghetti around your fork and then putting it in your mouth is the best method. You can also twirl the spaghetti into a spoon if one is provided. It is not acceptable to put one end of a noodle in your mouth and suck the rest in.

Food Allergies

In a restaurant where you are ordering from the menu, you can explain any allergies discreetly to your waitperson. Be pleasant and don't call attention to yourself or make this a topic of conversation.

Seasoning your Food

It is an insult to the chef to season your food before tasting it. Try a bite first, and then season it if necessary. Do not over season. This can appear childish.

Excusing Yourself from the Table

You can excuse yourself from the table by saying, "Excuse me;" you do not need to offer an explanation. If you must leave during the meal, you can indicate whether you are finished eating through proper placement of your utensils and napkin.

Men should rise when a lady leaves the table. It is not necessary to completely stand for a temporary departure. Men should rise off the seat to acknowledge her leaving.

The Check

When everyone has finished eating, you (or the table host) may catch the eye of the waitperson and say, "Check, please." Scan it for mistakes. If an error is found, signal your waitperson and quietly point out the error. Your waitperson will make the adjustment and return with a corrected check. In no circumstance should you make a scene.

If you are hosting the meal and paying for all the diners, do not display the total. Put the money (or signed form if paying by credit card) quietly into the payment booklet and nod to your waitperson to remove it. If you are paying with cash and do not have the exact amount, including the tip, wait for the waiter to bring the change, but if the sum includes both bill and tip, thank your waitperson and indicate that you are ready to leave by rising.

Splitting the Check

The best way of doing this is to ask for separate checks before you order. If your party is five or less people, this causes very little problem. However, in a larger group, separate checks are a nuisance for the waitperson which is why some restaurants have a policy of not giving separate checks to large groups. If everyone has chosen items that cost approximately the same, the best thing to do is ask each person for the same amount. But if some had only a soup and salad, for example, while others dined on steak and lobster, you should make appropriate allowances. Use a small calculator to make it easy.

Toasting

Toasting is a ritual to honor a person or an event. For example, a toast can be for a special guest or for newlyweds. Guests raise their glasses of wine, champagne, water (or whatever they are drinking) to honor the person or persons. If you are called on to lead the toast, here are some tips:

- The best time to toast is prior to the meal.
- The second best time to toast is just before dessert.
- Do NOT clink a glass for attention. Stand up and announce that you are about to offer a toast.
- It is acceptable to raise an empty glass for a toast.
- If you feel awkward giving a toast, simply say exactly what you feel. You can get away something as brief as "To George, you are the best." Or "To Sharon—a wonderful friend and great boss."

The person replying to the toast does not rise or drink the toast. That person should say "Thank You," and nod in the direction of the speaker. An option is to raise her glass in the direction of the speaker in a gesture of "Thanks, and here's to you, too."

Chapter 14. Formal Dining at Someone's Home

You have been invited to a formal dinner at a lovely home. It could be your boss or someone important that you want to impress. Follow these tips to make a positive impression on your host and the other guests.

Before the Dinner

When you get a written or e-mailed invitation, check your schedule and R.S.V.P. as soon as possible. R.S.V.P. are letters that stand for the French Respondez S'il Vous Plait which means "respond, if you please." Responding is a courtesy to let your hosts plan for the meal.

When You Arrive

First of all, do not arrive early. Your host may still be dressing or hurrying to get dinner ready. Arrive 10-15 minutes after the invitation time. Arriving later than 15 minutes is taboo because it is inconsiderate of your hosts. Do not show up with children unless the invitation says children are invited.

Do not arrive empty handed, but check with your host first to get the okay before bringing food or wine to accompany the meal. They may have already planned a special menu and your selection may not go with the meal.. Safer gifts to take are flowers, wine for the host to drink on another occasion, an inspirational book or anything that is thoughtful. This assumes the dinner party is small—less than 12 people. If you do take a gift, give it to your host or hostess as soon as you arrive. If you send it later, be sure to do it as soon as possible.

Sometimes it is better not to take a gift at all to a larger formal dinner—especially if you do not know the host well. It may not be customary among their friends; and you will only embarrass your host and other guests who have not brought a gift.

When Dinner is Announced

When dinner is announced, don't ignore the invitation. On the other hand, don't jump up and fly out as if you have been kept waiting to the point of starvation. Wait until the host or hostess is seated before you sit down. Wait until the host or hostess starts to eat before you eat, unless the host is not ready to eat yet and says, "Please begin."

During the Meal

At formal dinners it is **mandatory** that you talk to both of your neighbors. Even if you are seated next to someone for whom you have little interest, be considerate of your host. Do not ignore that person. Make a pretense, even for just a few minutes, of talking together. (See Chapter 5. Small Talk With Strangers)

If you don't see it, don't ask for it. If the host serves white dinner rolls and you prefer whole wheat, do not ask. If you like steak sauce on your steak, but none is on the table, do not ask.

At formal dinners guests should not ask for second helpings. If dishes are passed a second time, everyone is free to help themselves, even though others may not.

Unpleasant Conversation

Is anything more unpleasant than a conversation at a dinner table, where everyone is talking about a subject for which you have the opposite position? For example, what if you are a New York Mets fan and the conversation is pro-New York Yankee and anti-Mets. What if you are at the opposite side of a political or religious discussion?

One rule is to not argue at the table. Another rule is you should not leave the table in disgust. It is always important to remember that you do not want to embarrass your host and you do not want to burn any bridges. You have choices. One choice is to smile and say, "You know, my mama told me never to talk politics or religion, especially at a meal. I have stretched that to include sports. Do you mind if I stay out of this discussion?" No matter how much you may get prodded after that, just smile and keep quiet or use the broken record approach of repeating, "My mama told me…"

Another approach, which is admittedly painful, is to say nothing. Enjoy the food, try not to show your discomfort, finish your meal and leave as soon as possible. You don't want to win a battle and lose a war. Arguing may allow you to vent your feelings, but it could come back to bite you.

After the Meal

Guests do not put their napkins on the table until their hostess does. Once you have decided it is time to go, say thank you and good-bye to your hosts and LEAVE. Do not overstay your welcome. Afterwards, send a note to thank your host or hostess for the invitation and the wonderful meal.

Chapter 15. Other Meals

Job Interviews over a Meal

Besides being interviewed for your competency for a potential position in a company, you will be judged for your table manners. Wouldn't it be awful if you were the most qualified person for a job, but you blew it because you unwittingly made a major goof? Here are some tips that may help avoid that situation.

By reading the entire chapter on Dining, you already know which water glass and bread plate are yours. You know how to use your napkin. You know how to turn down wine, and much more. Job interviews have three major factors you should apply.

First of all, let your interviewer order first. If she insists you order first, feel free to ask her what she is going to have and order accordingly. Otherwise, play it safe and order a mid-range priced entrée. Try to avoid having your meal cost more than hers. You will have your first major goof if your host orders a salad for around $13.00 and you order prime rib for $29.00.

Secondly, order food that is easy to eat and not sloppy. Spaghetti is a definite mistake. You will be talking during your interview and don't want food that could mess up your clothes or is difficult to eat neatly.

Third, do not drink alcohol. If your interviewer orders wine and you love wine, by all means have a glass. But keep it to one or two glasses at the most. Being tipsy does not make a positive impression. I would avoid all other alcoholic drinks, even if your interviewer orders a few drinks.

Hosting a Barbeque

According to *Amy Vanderbilt Complete Book of Etiquette*, it is a good idea to tell your guests that they will be eating outdoors so that they can dress accordingly. In addition, keep a supply of shawls and sweaters for anyone who forgets to bring one. Let your guests know, too, how formal or informal the party will be; dress can vary from shorts to long country skirts.

Potluck Dinners

In certain parts of the country, covered dish or potluck dinners are very popular. If you are hosting a potluck dinner, you provide the setting, cocktails, coffee, and often a main dish. The wine could be your responsibility, but if someone in the group is a real connoisseur, that person can bring the wine. Creative hosts have a theme for the dinner, such as Italian, French, Chinese, Soul Food, etc. Your invitation should make it clear that all guests are to contribute to the meal.

If you are invited to a potluck dinner, you must R.S.V.P. (or send regrets), so that the host knows whether to expect you or not. You can take hors d'oeuvres, a first course, vegetables, casserole, salad, potatoes or rice, rolls, and dessert. Take your food in an attractive container, ideally one that can go from refrigerator to oven or stove, and onto the table.

For more information on dining, see Appendix A, Menu Items which is a glossary for dining, and Appendix B, More Dining Tips.

Chapter 16. Conclusion

My friend and editor, Susan Ely, gave the best reason for the importance of etiquette/manners. Susan quotes Margaret Walker who said, "Friends and good manners will take you where money won't go." Susan adds, "Manners will help you make those friends.

I hope you found my book informative and fun. Refer to it often to ensure that you will always be poised and confident in all social situations.

Thank you!

Appendix A. Menu Items

A la Carte	In the style of the menu. Each part of a meal or dish, such as soup, salad, extra cheese on a sandwich, etc. is individually priced. A la carte meals usually cost more than meals that are listed under one price.
Amandine	"With Almonds," often used in Chinese and fish dishes
Antipasto	Italian for appetizer
Au gratin	Served with bread crumbs and/or cheese on top
Au jus	In its own juices
Aupoivre	French, "with pepper"
Béarnaise	French, a heavy sauce consisting of eggs yolks, butter wine vinegar, tarragon, thyme, and shallots served over eggs or meat
Bisque	French, a thick cream soup consisting of shellfish and pieces
Bordelaise	French, a red wine sauce consisting of shallots, butter, tomatoes, onions and beef marrow
Bouillon	Clear broth
Brie	Semi soft cheese
Brochette	French for "skewer"
Caesar Salad	Salad made of Romaine lettuce, Parmesan cheese, olive oil, egg, lemon, spices, and sometimes anchovies that is usually tossed at your table
Camembert	A pungently flavored semi soft cheese
Canapés	French, an appetizer consisting of small pieces of bread topped with various spreads
Cappuccino	An Italian coffee made of hot milk and strong black coffee
Champignons	French for "mushrooms"
Chateaubriand	French, a thick cut of grilled sirloin or Porterhouse steak served with vegetables and sauce
Consommé	Clear, seasoned broth
Cordon Bleu	Swiss for "blue ribbon." Items stuffed or served with Swiss cheese
Croissant	Crescent-shaped French roll

Crudités	French, an appetizer of raw vegetables
Du Jour	French for "of the day," such as "soup du jour"
En croute	French for "in a crust"
Entrée	French for "main course"
Escargots	French for "snails"
Fettuccine	Italian ribbon noodles
Filet Mignon	French for a small, thick steak from the beef tenderloin
Flambé	French for "flamed"
Florentine	A French cooking style in which food is served on spinach and topped with a cream sauce and grated cheese
Fondue	Swiss style of dipping food into a hot pot of oil or cheese with special forks
Fromage	French for "cheese"
Half-shell	Raw shellfish served with a sauce
Hollandaise	A rich sauce of egg yolks, butter, lemon, and vinegar
Hors d'oeuvres	Appetizers
Julienne	Meat or vegetables cut into sticks or shreds
Lait	French for "milk"
Legumes	French for "vegetables"
Mornay	French, a sauce with of butter, flour, broth, cream, and cheese
Mousse	A French dish with a smooth, whipped texture, as in "chocolate mousse"
Nicoise	French, with tomatoes and garlic and possibly black olives, onions, and peppers
Nouilles	French for "noodles"
Pain	French for "bread"
Patisserie	French for "pastry"
Petit-fours	French for "little cakes"
Poisson	French for "fish"
Potage	French soup
Poulet	French "chicken"
Prawn	Large shrimp

Prosciutto	Italian, salted but not cooked ham
Provencale	French, cooked with tomatoes, garlic, and olive oil
Quiche Lorraine	French, a tart consisting of cream, eggs, cheese, and bacon
Roquefort	Blue cheese
Roti	French for "roasted"
Salisbury steak	A patty of ground beef
Saumon	French for "salmon"
Sauté	To cook quickly in fat
Sorbet	French for "sherbet." A tart ice
Soufflé	French for "puffed up." A baked dish of whipped eggs and flavorings. Tip: Order soufflé 20 minutes before dessert course.
Steak Diane	Thin steak sautéed or flamed in butter and sherry at your table
Steak Tartare	Raw ground beef that has been ground twice, had seasonings added, and is topped with a raw egg
Veau	French for "veal"
Viande	French for "meat"
Vichyssoise	A cold cream, chicken stock, leek and potato soup
Vinaigrette	An oil and vinegar dressing
Vin	French for "wine"
Vin blanc	French for "white wine"
Vin rouge	French for "red wine"

Appendix B. More Dining Tips

Dining Do's

If you are a slow eater, try to stay with the pace of the meal so that you don't hold up the remaining courses. If you are lagging behind, when the others are done eating, don't make them wait on you too long.

When drinking iced tea or coffee, limit yourself to one or two packets of sugar. Tear one or both at the same time ¾ of the way at the top of the packet, and leave the paper waste at the side of the plate. Using more than two packets of sugar or artificial sweetener may be seen as excessive.

If your waitperson brings you the wrong thing, you can discreetly mention immediately so that it can be corrected. If the error is small – you didn't want onions, but they are served to you, or you received the wrong side dish, ignore it. Fussing over food can make you look childish, finicky and concerned with the wrong things. Your goal is to always appear gracious.

To avoid certain foods that you don't like (like onions), discreetly eat around the food and/or move it carefully to the side of the plate or bowl. Do not make a fuss, and don't remove it from the plate. If someone asks, "How is your meal?" be polite and say, "Fine, thank you."

If your food is cold or doesn't taste good, you should just eat it and not cause a scene. However, if it is not edible, politely call your waitperson and explain.

You do not have to clean your plate. It is polite to leave some food on your plate. Do not push the remaining food around the plate.

Dining Don'ts

Do not lick your fork or spoon after your remove the utensil from your mouth.

Do not take partial bites off a utensil; and do not put more food on your fork or spoon than you can place in your mouth with one bite.

Do not use eye drops or apply lipstick at the table. No grooming of any kind should be done at the table. You should excuse yourself for this purpose.

Don't lean back and announce, "I'm through," or "Whew, I'm stuffed." The fact that you have put your eating utensils in the proper position shows you are finished eating.

Don't ever put liquid into your mouth if it is already filled with food. You might have a little piece of bread in your mouth when you take a drink, if it is so small no one can see it. Otherwise, don't do it.

Don't wipe off the silverware in a restaurant. If you do happen to find a dirty piece of silverware at your place, call your waitperson, show him the soiled spoon or fork, and ask for a new one.

Don't crook your pinkie finger when picking up your cup. It looks silly and pretentious.

Don't leave your spoon in your coffee cup. Not only does it look unattractive; it is almost certain to result in an accident.

Don't leave half of the food on your spoon or fork to be waved about during conversation.

Don't cut up your entire meal before you start to eat; it only makes a mess on your plate.

Don't pile mashed potatoes and peas on top of the meat on your fork — just don't take huge mouthfuls of any food.

Index

S

T

U

V

W